THE WEE TREASURY OF

PRAISES OF MIDDLE AGE: MEDITATIONS ON THINGS THAT WILL GO WRONG

WRITTEN BY MARSTON LYONS

Copyright © 2021 by Marston Lyons

All rights reserved. This book or any portion thereof may not be reproduced or used in any manner whatsoever without the express written permission of the publisher except for the use of brief quotations in a book review.

Printed in the United States of America

ISBN: 978-1-7378044-4-4

www.MarstonLyons.com

Why I Wrote This Book

I wrote this book in response to my body's ever-evolving physical and emotional status as the days, months, and years pass through it.

They say with age comes wisdom. Over time, I've learned that optimism is the best medicine. So now, whenever my body presents me with some new age-related milestone, my immediate volley back is the same eternal sunshine and lollipops that have brought me through life thus far.

I thought I'd share my unyielding middle-age enthusiasm with you as well. Hopefully, you will appreciate these counterarguments and perhaps turn your point of view on aging towards sunshine and lollipops, too.

Now, go find your glasses, if they're not already on your head, and get to your chair.

Table of Contents

Why I Wrote This Book..iii

Section One: Metabolism Slows Down
(Stockpiling Your Energy Reserve).....1

Section Two: Looks Fading (Aging With
Grace and/or Dignity) 23

Section Three: Low Motivation
(Indifference Is Bliss) 35

Section Four: Ailments
(New Mysteries Unfold) 41

Section Five: No Longer a Target Demographic
for Anything Cool (We Can Think
for Ourselves) 67

Section Six: Corporate Prison (Job Security)....... 79

Section Seven: Debts (Helping the Economy) 85

Section Eight: Isolation (Silent Lucidity) 91

Section Nine: The End (The Beginning
of the Next Chapter) 99

Section Ten: Middle Age in Summary................103

About the Author 107

SECTION ONE:

Metabolism Slows Down (Stockpiling Your Energy Reserve)

Weight Gain

Thank goodness my body cares so much about my survival that it insists on hugging me with a thick, warm layer of fat to keep me safe and nourished.

Weight

Your new fat energy reserves make it easier to throw your weight around. You are consistently becoming more impressive, and you can stand your ground effortlessly.

Gain Weight by Looking at Food?

Behold! Your body is a complicated and mysterious machine, powered by evolution and genetics and your environment. We have no further information for you at this time, other than this: proceed with caution and take good notes for your next doctor's visit.

Food Is the Comfort and the Problem

A double-edged sword—you are what you eat: soft and mushy and full of fat.

Trying to Stay Healthy, but It Gets More Difficult

God doesn't give you more than you can handle, unless it comes to the bathroom scale.

Slower Metabolism

Enjoy slowing down because you have spent your whole life in the rat race! Your body is slowing down to give you more incentive to relax and think about the simple things in life, like where you put your keys.

Have to Eat Healthier, Less Appealing Foods

Thank goodness your taste buds these days are more utilitarian so that you can tolerate your morning bowl of bland fibrous roughage, which will enable you to empty your bowels regularly.

New Priorities that Get You Moving

Your morning constitutional is starting to become so important that you will nearly salivate at the thought of a dry, dense bran muffin. More prune juice? Yes, please! It's nature's answer to a murky, syrupy beverage.

Can't Eat Like You Used To

Remember all the days you could have pizza for breakfast, cookies for lunch, and eat dinner in a diner at two am? Good thing you can still remember those times. Are you sure you were there and that wasn't something on TV? Ok, just checking.

A Ray of Sunshine

So happy I can finally clean up my diet now that I've learned my body can no longer process appealing food that tastes good.

SECTION TWO:

Looks Fading
(Aging With Grace and/or Dignity)

Beauty

Looks aren't as important when you age because you are now more focused on wondering where they went.

Form Follows Function Fashions

"Practical" and "forgiving" are two buzzwords in your fashion world these days. Clothes are less distracting and more comfortable now, so it's easier to feel like you're wearing pajamas all the time.

Hair Don'ts

Why complicate life with an exhausting hairstyle routine? People are more likely to be entranced by your "it fits, it's clean and it's comfortable" clothes style.

Embarrassed to be Seen in a Swimsuit?

Join the club! Now is your time to find a modest swimming garment that maintains your modesty, hides saggy cellulite, shields your skin from UV rays and has at least some bit of appealing style. Good luck finding it in your size or a in a flattering color, though!

A Timeless Curiosity

Being middle aged gives you a pass to wear just about anything you want in public, as long as you aren't trying to wear something designed for a younger generation. Then, you'd better run for cover!

A Timeless Curiosity

Being middle aged gives you a pass to wear just about anything you want in public, as long as you aren't trying to wear something designed for a younger generation. Then, you'd better run for cover!

SECTION THREE:

Low Motivation
(Indifference Is Bliss)

A Hectic Schedule

Your new clock is not only just "work hours" and "after work hours," the clock now also includes "before dinner hours" and "after dinner hours." "After dinner hours" are further subdivided into "before recliner hours" and "actual recliner hours." Once "actual recliner hours" have begun any task that comes up during that time must be weighed very carefully to see if it is worth getting up out of your recliner for or not.

A Moment of Clarity

Learn not to look so closely in the mirror anymore. Fortunately, by the grace of God, you can't see yourself in the mirror very closely anymore—without the aid of eyeglasses, that is. And who has that kind of time? You need to get back to your chair. Your show is on.

SECTION FOUR:

Ailments
(New Mysteries Unfold)

The Gift of Gab

There is always something new to talk about and share with those around you and anyone else you meet by the ACE bandage wrap section of the store.

Keep Your Sherlock Holmes Hat Nearby—There's a New Health Mystery Every Day!

With age comes wisdom. Improve your knowledge base by becoming a Google MD and learn all the fascinating health things that can go wrong between now and the finish line.

The Momentum Continues to Build

Remember way back, when you were merely concerned about your newly discovered tinnitus? Now, that's just background noise compared to all the other health curiosities (real or imagined) that you may or may not have cropping up!

Memory Fading

You always feel like you are hearing new information. In fact, you'll soon feel like you could earn an advanced degree with all the new information you keep learning about again and again.

Subjective Diligence

You need repetition to make sure new information sinks in, so keep asking the same questions like a persistent reporter. Your busy brain is multitasking, so let's be a bit more understanding.

Forgetful

You can't be expected to remember everything. That's why there's the internet.

Up All Night (In the Bathroom)

What good night's rest doesn't include at least two bathroom break intermissions? Time to stretch your legs and stay active. Old age won't slow me down!

Imagining a Diagnosis

What's that lump? What's that bump? What's that pain? What's that strain? Answer to each: "Oh great universe, is this the beginning of the end?" Review your life goals and create a timeline. Repeat for every ailment, new or imagined, that comes your way.

Be the Grasshopper

Plan ahead! Start stockpiling your medical equipment stash: crutches, a portable wheelchair, splints, harnesses, a cane, ACE wrap, hot packs, a toilet riser. You never know when you will need them. Best to just start using them all now to save time.

Getting to Know You

Needing an earlier bedtime makes you less interest in going out anywhere late (within two hours of your early bedtime). This freed up evening schedule gives you plenty of time for internal reflection, internal monologue, and ideas for a book.

New Talents Abound

If you're lucky, one day, your trick knee might turn into one of those rain forecasting knees that some of the cooler seniors have.

A Breath of Fresh Air

Don't think of it as "never having cheese again." Think of it as "not being up all night with painful and persistent explosive gas."

SECTION FIVE:

No Longer a Target Demographic for Anything Cool
(We Can Think for Ourselves)

No Longer Cool

Although you are no longer "cool," you are often cold! Grab a sweater or you'll catch a chill. Unless you are undergoing hormonal changes that make you hot all the time, then staying cool is at the top of your list.

Pop Culture?

You are at the stage where you think everything nowadays is just a copycat of the same bad song/movie/tv show. But gather round children and let me tell you about the magic of Kajagoogoo and Mork from Ork!

A Homecoming

It's finally your time to become that grouchy old man or cantankerous old woman that you laughed about in your youth. "Get off my lawn" and "What did you say?" are your new catchphrases. Congratulations—you've come full circle!

Kids of Today

You see the younger generation as life choice mistakes waiting to happen. Feel free to impart them with your sage advice, wisdom, and guidance from your life experience thus far. Note: Be prepared for them to not listen, understand, or care.

No Longer a Target Demographic

Our mature generation is too sophisticated to be labeled as fun, carefree, thrill seeking, impulsive, or other ways the younger generations are labeled by advertisements. We are intelligent, and we can think for ourselves about what movies look good or what cereals to eat. Pro tip: if companies are trying to sell retro eighties anything and/or something that contains bran, we will probably buy it.

Section Six:

Corporate Prison
(Job Security)

You Still Got It!

You're not that old. In fact, you're too young to retire! Yes, you still need to be in the rat race for another decade or two—depending on how much you want to earn from Social Security—if Social Security will still be available by the time you retire.

Patience Is a Virtue

If retirement is the finish line to a lifetime of trying to stockpile money, then you can't afford to retire yet. Not for a long, long time.

Section Seven:

Debts
(Helping the Economy)

Thankful

Thank God I have my debts to keep me grounded. I feel needed, valued, and appreciated—by the bill collectors, that is.

One Small Step for Man

Debts are like little achievements; each month that you can pay them, you've accomplished something amazing!

Section Eight:

Isolation
(Silent Lucidity)

More "Me" Time

With fewer reasons to leave the house, you now have more time to explore your thoughts, meditate, and mentally steer "the ship of you."

Deep Thoughts

Make doubly duty use of the time you spend on housework and paying your debts (and earning money to pay these debts) by pondering a philosophical perspective on this great riddle of the universe. Or you can just skip the housework and watch YouTube.

Missed Opportunities

Get creative...you now have more time on your hands to relive the moments in your life where you might have chosen a different path. Have fun imagining the endless possible outcomes!

SECTION NINE:

The End
(The Beginning of the Next Chapter)

A Pattern of Infinity

Each new day is one day closer to learning the answer to the great riddle of the universe. Each new day is also a day to try and finally catch up on washing the dishes.

SECTION TEN:

Middle Age in Summary

In summary,

In middle age:

- **Metabolism slows down**
- **Looks fade**
- **Low motivation**
- **Ailments**
- **No longer target demographic for anything cool**
- **Corporate prison**
- **Debts**
- **Isolation**
- **The end**

OR.....

In summary:

MIDDLE AGE:

- Stockpiling your energy reserve
- Aging with grace and/or dignity
- Indifference is bliss
- New mysteries unfold
- We can think for ourselves
- Job security
- Helping the economy
- Silent lucidity
- The beginning of the next chapter

Now, doesn't that feel better?

About the Author

I have been a purveyor of humor since the third grade. Since that time, I have quietly honed my humorous view of life as a coping skill for whatever path I walked on. Fortunately, there was plenty to laugh about along the way—most notably, it was my grade school impromptu performance art of "Alien Hand Syndrome," which was inspired by "The Weekly World News (and made my mom and sister laugh so much with many command performances requested). Despite being told by my high school science class lab partner, "You're not funny, you know," my humorous ways persisted.

I unexpectedly became aware that I was a humor writer when I took a poetry class in New York City. As I read aloud what I thought were deep and poignant thoughts, scattered laughter sprang up from multiple sources in the classroom around me. Although crushed and hotly embarrassed, I went along with my haunting scribbles as being deliberately humorous—and then enrolled in a TV sitcom writing class instead.

I later developed a laughter-through-anxiety writing method while I struggled to find a way to survive alone in New York City in a low-paying entry-level publishing job. From this traumatic experience, my first book was written/born: How to Survive and Thrive in New York on $19,000* a Year (*or Less) Before Taxes.

My writing reawakened after having children, and I found it was a quiet, relaxing, and affordable outlet for me. I was thrilled when I had some humorous essays published online and flattered when they were subsequently published in a book. I created the blog "Fortyteen Candles" about a decade ago, which helped me learn how to quickly craft an essay. That blog made me proud because I learned I could connect with other people through my writing.

Since then, while muddling through the inertia of the 9–5 grind, I have finally accepted that creativity is what makes me feel most content. The writings I create are therapeutic and healing for me. I hope you can relate to my books and find something in them that makes you feel happy as well!

> Take care,
> Marston Lyons

**Other Books by Marston Lyons
in "The Wee Treasury" Book Series:**

The Wee Treasury of Alternative Swear Options for New Parents....and for Those who Want to Keep it Mild

And more titles on the way!

www.ingramcontent.com/pod-product-compliance
Lightning Source LLC
Chambersburg PA
CBHW070926080526
44589CB00013B/1438